CW00519864

# TAKING FLIGHT

# TAKING FLIGHT

## KATHRYN DASZKIEWICZ

Shoestring Press

All rights reserved. No part of this work covered by the copyright
hereon may be reproduced or used in any means – graphic, electronic,
or mechanical, including copying, recording, taping, or information
storage and retrieval systems – without written permission of the
publisher.

Printed by imprintdigital
Upton Pyne, Exeter
www.imprintdigital.net

Typeset by narrator
www.narrator.me.uk
enquiries@ narrator.me.uk

Published by Shoestring Press
19 Devonshire Avenue, Beeston, Nottingham, NG9 1BS
(0115) 925 1827
www.shoestringpress.co.uk

First published 2012
© Copyright: Kathryn Daszkiewicz

The moral right of the author has been asserted.

ISBN 978 1 907356 50 6

# ACKNOWLEDGEMENTS

Acknowledgements are due to the editors of the following publications and websites where some of these poems first appeared: *Acumen, The Bow-Wow Shop, Critical Survey, The Frogmore Papers, 14 Magazine, The Interpreter's House, Poetry International.org, Prole, Smiths Knoll* and *Staple*.

# CONTENTS

*For John*

# PALAEONTOLOGY

*"It is well known that people with dementia are continually absorbed by the past.
That means they can still recall the past vividly. The information from the past
remains accessible the longest. They sometimes experience the past as the present."*
*Dementia in Close-Up*, Bère. M. L. Miesen

## I *Blue Lias*

In the Blue Lias that is your head
layers of marl, clay and limestone
succumb to wave and gale.
In time, they crumble.

> And the small bleeds
> > forcing their way on the inside
> > > are the treacherous springs
> > > > which thrust the fossil past

> > > to overlay the parts of you
> we tried to unearth
> only yesterday.

## II *Brittle Stars*

So slender, the arms of Brittle Stars,

> it's rare to find one whole.

> > So your words falter and fragment,

sink under sediment.

We take them back home in our heads

to tap and tap

at the hapless overlap:

       those decades of despairing

arms flung wide.

## III  Xenoliths

Stranger stones
       by magma thrust
           from earth's deep crust
       into a vulnerable present
allow geologists
       to probe the past.

Time is in schism
       as granite gives way
to anachronism.

I melt into my mother
       or your aunt.

## IV  Belemnites

*God's thunderbolts*
folk said. Hurled
from the heights in storms
to wound the earth.
Their javelin shapes
lodged deep.

That they could be
internal shells of molluscs
built for speed
and then destroyed –
sheer heresy.

You used to be so sharp.

2

## V  Ichthyosaurus

When you first started to forget it was
*easier to pretend it was a crocodile*
easier to put it down to old age – a memory lapse
*ignore the serpent neck, those limbs like paddles*
when keys conspired against you and your tie became unfathomable
*than to see God's hand receding like the flood*
dismantling Creation.

## VI  Ammonites

Your brain closes on itself
like a serpent stone. Its chambers
calcify. We trace the sutures with expectant fingers;
but what was knowledge –
forbidden or otherwise –
is banished. Fled, without
St Hilda's whip.

## VII  Horsetail Ferns

Some species grow
on land that's been laid waste;
ground which has been disturbed.

These ferns have silica crystals
in their stems, so Boy Scouts
use them to scour dirty pots.

Their fossil ancestors, the calamites,
were huge – and thrived
four hundred million years ago.

So echoes of the past
have been preserved through aeons
of calamitous change.

My broad palms hold
the strength and shape of yours.
Your hand's still in my hand.

# GRASS

When your mind, meticulous as a map,
led us down lanes no one else knew
where grasses reached new heights,

I thought it nothing to wind the window down
and with one jubilant sweep
strip off their seeds, then watch

the random breeze disorder
all that had composed
their graceful heads.

# NIL BY MOUTH

Another stroke, and, as if it were a bird
your swallow vanishes. Flies off

at the start of a bleak season
on the blue scythe of its wings.

Your mind, flitting across some other
sky, is closed to us, our futile

bedside twitterings, is perched
on a cusp between worlds

seeking finer air. While
the dark screen of poplars beyond

the hospital window
obscures our view

of heaven.

# LOSING TOUCH

It's three years since you died, but longer
since dementia's poison spread and you receded
like Eurydice to a place we couldn't go,
and we could only watch as you yielded to the pull
of a muddy past, while in the present keys
turned traitor in your hands and your brain
was a cell phone of random connections –
a game of noughts and crosses nobody
could win. The toaster, you insisted,
must be plugged in so you could use the landline.
You wondered why you couldn't call us
that time the dog – who sensed things weren't right –
wouldn't come back: your 'mobile'
the TV remote control. And very soon
the only ones to reach you were those folk
you thought we were. As if you were already
on the other side.

# LEARNING TO WALK

You used to drive me to Newcastle Central,
point out the Tyne's weak bridge. But later
only to East Boldon station. The last time

I braved you at the wheel, when we were half
way down Moor Lane you turned: *Am I
taking you somewhere?* Now I have to walk.

I look across the tracks to where you warmed
your hands on the real coal fire as a schoolboy
in that bright green blazer I found yesterday

in these days of endless sorting. As ever, when
I look across the flats, a kestrel's hovering,
some vole or field mouse in its sights.

I know that it will swoop.

# SHIT CITY

Dismantling the home where
I was made and where you both
are not and yet appear in all that I

unearth is work that suffocates.
I head outside to where the Metro
loops its loop. Look at the map. Some

vandal, a Newcastle fan,  I guess,
has circled Sunderland in black. *Shit
City's* written boldly underneath. Spit

on a paper hanky dulls the edge. A
futile gesture. There could be
a YOU ARE HERE arrow. If

the yellow train should whiz me well
away to the airport or beyond I'd still
be floundering on that cold coast.

# NOT A CLOUD

That wouldn't be your style.
But the glint of a camera lens

in your favourite shop window
seems a little too bright on a day

when the sun is a broken promise.
And sometimes when I can't sleep

I could swear that Sirius winks.
Tonight in a January tantrum

you are the steady blur
of headlights through the rain.

And were I on the coast you would
– as time is nothing now –

be shining as the eye of Souter Point
before its beam was stilled.

# SELLING WEST MEADOWS ROAD

Because of the boy who played Icarus, that door stayed shut,
the staircase spiralling to nowhere. The Doric backdrop
had lent an elegance to his floundering until he hit the scrub.

Greek drama on a hill near Sunderland, at Penshaw Monument
- half sized replica of the Thesion, Temple of Hephaestus:
steel pins and brackets holding gritstone blocks in place.

Local folly, once visible from my parents' window
until the estate of Wimpey houses blocked Athens
from their sight. He was five - she, not yet born in 1926

when Temperley Arthur Scott, palms skimming the cold stone,
climbed up on Easter Monday, counting the steps and looking for the light.
And as a child that *when we first moved* view

was always myth to me. Once when we picnicked on the slope
I tried to guess which column hugged its mildewed secrets.
Years later, when I drove up from the south, it signalled home.

What is it now that all their rooms are closed to me?
Someone is sanding footfalls from those stairs I trod
a dozen times a day, handprints dissolving from the banister.

# THE NEW OWNERS

They have bricked up the fireplace
so the house can't breathe;
the lares will not stay without a hearth.

And as the wall which sealed warm spaces is knocked down
the searchlight sun exposes
what was intimate.

They have torn the pink rose from the trellis
dug out the maygold and the mermaid;
and as their scent was flailing in the air

flagged down the garden for a carport.
The oak door's natural grain is choked with grey
and the household snake

at home in its old skin
sloughs off the new
and slithers away through the boards.

# ON CLEADON HILLS

What my boots have crushed on this path that snakes beside
the barley field offers up the scent of sometime summers
all frock and grass-stained plimsoll under a more benevolent sun
as the wheels of a discarded bicycle whirred to a standstill.

Pineapple weed, whose tiny oval blooms bring the exotic
to a north east hillside, began somewhere far off as childhood,
where the desire to find a four leafed clover and to perform
the love-me love-me-not routine of plucking daisies,

was a chill breeze that came from a distant coast
set nodding the blousy meadowsweet, purple vetch,
stripped stars by the thousand from tired spires of rosebay
to the backdrop of the gaunt and sailless windmill.

# SHADOWS

The afternoons were always yellow then:
like centres of daisies which we picked
and chained on Auntie Grace's lawn
like the laburnum tree
which rained gold every May.

*Don't eat the pods*
*they're poisonous.*
My thumbnail is all green.
There is an echo when
I help Gran shell the Sunday peas.

*And Mr Thompson*
*must be there somewhere*
*behind those pink hydrangeas*
*he watered every evening with a hose.*
*They're flowering still and make a kind of sunset*
*against the primrose door*
*which never opens now.*

We will have lemonade when
*Watch with Mother's* on
I hope it is *The Wooden Tops* today
as Spotty Dog's my favourite
since our hamster went to Jesus.

*From the back bedroom we can see the sea*
*but not the beach*
*and not Trow Rocks*
*where the small boy was lured by the big lads*
*by promises of paddling and sand castles*
*and didn't know*
*about the ledge*
*that sucked the bathers*
*right out of their depth.*

*They only found his shoes.*

# HERE

there used to be fields: a horse or two
cropping grass among rosebay and buttercups;
greenhouses of a nursery called Groves;
its owner's house the shade of blackbird's eggs.

In the new estate the houses are detached
on roads called Thirlmere, Grasmere,
Windermere. They boast two cars apiece;
too many for the single garages.

It's still a right of way, but little green
is left. And on those days the summer sky is blue,
it's with remembered swallows.

# POST IMPRESSIONISM

Mr Lowe is so gangly
he could have splintered
long limb by long limb
from a triptych by El Greco.

Obsessed with green peppers
and sheep skulls, he plays
Emmylou Harris and Doobie Brothers
on a rickety turntable,

shows us creaky slides
of The Impressionists. *Thighs! Whoa
— thighs!* he roars as a lad next to the screen's
about to smirk at a porky Renoir nude.

Paper, he says, is precious.
One afternoon when he nips out
we raid his cupboard.
A pile of matchboxes teeters,

falls, unslots its treasure
of dried wasps across the tiles.
*Here, there and everywhere*
Emmylou trills as we scuffle

on hands and knees gleeful
and incredulous over the chequered floor;
freeze, like Escher leaves,
as the door edges open.

# ROOST

As the late cry of a blackbird ricochets
through the undergrowth at dusk you're
back in those green days, kicking
against the curfew, skin a criss-cross
of pressed grass where you knelt,
initiate in the mysteries of cuckoo spit
and afternoons stretched, a fat roll
of elastoplast, laborious as geometry
across a languid summer;
and as the day slid its head under
a dark wing, you tossed that last defiant stone
to skitter then fade into stillness,
until even you, nodding, found yourself
sinking toward the feathered insularity of sleep.

# THIN ICE

Kay Maria was always Irina Rodnina
while we fought over Diane Towler,
Sonja Henje and an unpronounceable
Protopopov. A semi-circle of pavement

in front of her cul-de-sac home
was our rink, the rubber wheels
of our grey leather skates
transforming into blades

as we rolled up to perform.
I can still hear the whir and trundle
when we skirted across cracks,
the screech at the kerb's

sudden danger. Feel the coarse
lichened wall against my legs
as we waited for Kay Maria
to announce our scores.

I'd traipse home licking blood
from my palms, the tang
of privet that had hedged my fall
still clinging to my skin.

At night the loops and glides
of those exotic names
would scar the frozen fabric of my sleep
until the thin ice gave.

# IN STARBUCKS

Across the table we regard
each other levelly as normality's
disfigured by a storm. Somewhere
a rush of air. A door swings open.
Of a sudden I am teetering
on the precipice of your stare.

With a thousand unexploded raindrops
the collapsed umbrella by the exit eyes us
as if deciding whether it's required
to do a Mary Poppins should I jump.

If you'd but grab the handle and my hand
and take off from this place. And when we're in mid air
thrust the canopy skyward with such force
an upwards shower of too-long-dormant drops

will meet and merge with those
bound for the earth. So let
the anything happen.

# BLUE TATTOO

Taut as a drum, you beat
a slow tattoo against my skin.
At each stroke, the gutteral utterance

that renders speech redundant;
at each stroke, blue worlds
mute as bruises. Boundaries

blur, as you ink out an indelible territory
where language is pure rhythm
and retreat no longer an option.

# HEAT

That time, going for gold,
    when speed and silence
were necessities, my eyes
    stayed on your face
just as we crossed
    the line: a replay
of a sprinter in slow
    motion. The blue
chaise longue was in
    on the conspiracy,
its smug bun feet
absorbing our abandon.
    Only the flame-red amaryllis
cried out in muted unison.

# HOARD

Your kiss on the top of my head
is the moon in daylight
pale token of small hours

when the air turned blue
with your sweet expletives –
currency I will spend again

and again in your absence
to bankrupt yet another
night of sleep.

# CLOSE

... and when your fingers interlock with mine,
I think of the hidden nests of harvest mice
in fields rife with cocksfoot or tufted hair grass,
or maybe somewhere on a brambled slope,
where shredded leaves are woven to a ball
with living ones pulled in, keeping the structure
taut; an inside cosy, lined with thistledown;
and when the little creatures come or go
they close the gap so there's no sign
that they were ever there, all summer long
between the flowering stems.

# LEAF DANCE

*'... but oh the sunshine has a fearful effect on me – it makes me want to take you
into a wood over the hill & undress you & kiss the leaf-shadows moving over your
body, & love you till you are quite quite dead.'*
Cecil Day-Lewis to Rosamond Lehmann

As the broad palms of the horse chestnut
laid claim to her whiteness he was
touched by their reverence – summer
candles held high as if to see her better.

Heart-shaped leaves of aspen
Chinese-whispered, of lovers
kissing in the grasses. The impotent ash
could only jangle last year's keys.

Now, as bare trees vein the sky
he is taunted by evergreens which fail
to screen a watery winter sun.
And the leaf between

the pages of the book which he slid
laughing from her hands that day
floats from its chapter, a brittle ghost.
And what once danced is stilled.

# MIDDLE MANAGEMENT

When your guilt wears thin, then
I'm the gold you mine for. But
most of the time you hug it
uxoriously to your soul like
lead – a grim ballast that
threatens to upend all three
of us. And if I think of you and me
as merely friends, I picture
the last scene of that film where a bus
is teetering on a cliff edge. And though
the criminals know what's throwing
it off balance – it's something that
may well have tipped too far.

# 'BACHELOR'

He dispensed
with the sidecar,
left it back home
(with the wife
and two-point-four)
burnt rubber
on the side
roads. Almost
undone by
a telltale hairpin
bend.

      Dandelions
on the verge clocked
the hours he played
away. Fireworked
their spurious seeds
in mocking mimicry.

A September breeze
fleet as a rumour
swept a spiteful few
to dog his wake.

Next summer
they will shake
their brazen manes
in the bed
he dug himself
desecrating
the dahlias.

# DON'T DIE IN EGYPT

Don't die in Egypt - the jackal
headed god who has plucked out
so many hearts would fear that yours
might choke Ammit the gobbler
who part croc, part leopard, with some
hippopotamus thrown in
is loitering by the scales.

No spectacular sins -
well, maybe one or two - just
the conglomeration of small
acts of cruelty which furred
then hardened round that vital part,
like a kettle whose element clogged
with limescale is incapable of warmth.

Tourist, despite the fact
that looking out for number one
was second nature, you'd be ignorant
of the scarab carved from nemehef
inscribed with spells to stop
a telltale heart from owning up
to all its crimes.

The powers waive the negative
confession. Maat's ostrich feather
stays in her hand. For you came forth
from a cold place heading west.
And were deaf to the signs of love.

# TO BE CONTINUED

Along a lime-lined road,
past an overgrown pillbox,

(remnant of Stop Line Red)
we wandered in the heat

until we found the grave
where only lichen bloomed.

It was a heady day
that promised sunshine

but clouds suppressed it
to a suffocating simmer.

Watched by the yellow eyes
of a thousand unspent pennymoons

we retreated through an avenue
of trees we could not name.

# TIGER IN WAITING

Then, for all I knew, feng shui
might have gone well with noodles.
Our room faced north. I couldn't
see the door. At night, thick curtains
kept a flickering road at bay. Shut out
The Plough. I was water to your fire.
By day a telegraph pole, close to the house,
shot poison chi across the big sash window.

I moved south - across the landing. Now
on windy nights I watch the birch tree
toss its glittering fleece, the energy
in free flow. In the distant hills perhaps
a dragon sleeps, while open blinds invite
auspicious stars to spell a future where
alone's not lonely. A thrush calls from the ash.
It is the single birds who sing the most.

# ANNIVERSARY

How apt, that, twenty years to the day
I should be making my own way over
the fens, flat field by flat field. Leafless
Lombardy poplars reach for clouds
and fail while wind farms slice the air:
new age waders all leg and cruel beak.

I can not hate the bleakness now
I am not the heron waiting on the bank
for something to silver the dull shallows.

# MEWS

'And whereas the Muses had been their own mistresses, the goddesses were now
declared to be servants of the Greeks' own god of inspiration, Apollo.'
'Before she was an artefact of culture, the muse was a natural force...'
The Goddess Path – Patricia Monaghan

'Falconry's appeal was based on such factors as the spectacular nature of the falcon's
stoop, the drama and uncertainty of the hawk's hunt, the power of being able to
recall a free flying wild creature and the knowledge that the practice of the sport was
an indicator of membership in the social elite.'
The Kings and Their Hawks – Falconry in Medieval England – Robin S.
Oggins

## I  What's in a Name

The kestrel is Euterpe but here she is not glad. And though
Calliope, the gyrfalcon, is not fair voiced, she tells us tales

of daring and true flight when we're in moult. Thalia – now
she is aptly named! She clowns and makes us laugh. Urania

is aloof but cannot see the stars - not through this shingled roof.
She glares at Terpsichore who shuffles on her perch and tings

her silver bells. Polymnia, Clio and Erato are seeled and not yet manned.
Melpomene the peregrine – who sulks – dreams of the lureless dive.

He was inspired to name us thus, our lord. But the austringer
begged leave to call the haggard what he chose. He is little read.

Tisiphone. We put our faith in her. She preens and bides her time.

## II  *Taking Flight*

The exhilaration
of the kill
of nailing it
in one swift blow
was all our own. Now
there's the invisible
elastic of the lure
as he, without the bite
of beak  or talon
on surrogate wings
plays at god.

One swing
and like Icarus
we return
to the ignominous earth
of his fist.

## III  *Manning*

No food. No sleep.
No light. Eyelids sewn up –
seeled tight. Feet stayed
by jesses through
a varvel threaded.
Talons blunted
then on a fist
ignobly shunted
from dark to dark
and back a day, a night.
And when she's fed
after so long –
conditioned

to a bar of song
which equals food.

*IV Rhythm*

The French call us *rowers*
because our rapid wingbeats scull

the air. While hawks are *sailors* –
they fan their tails and soar.

We dive and strike our quarry in mid
flight. A hawk stays hidden

surprises from below. Its feet
grip tight to wring the meaning out.

*V Haggard*

The size of a tiercel,
his strength, his span
of ours a mere third.

And so it is that we are
prised from the wild
more often. Bound

for the air brought
low. We, who could
put the wind to rights

beneath our wings
and grip a living branch
beneath our feet,

exchange this
for a cadge
and curse

of a falconer's glove.

## VI Quill

In this prison of mutes
and moult (only in perfect
plumage may we hunt,
so are confined) the fountain's
sound is distant. It spews
stale water from the brazen
heads of leopards. Can we
compose ourselves?
Our flight feathers grow
straight. These quills
are not our own.

## VII End of Our Tether

It serves him right – in spite
of all of his secondhand

attempts at flight
clichés are all that's left.

We won't beat about the bush.
Hoodwinked for all those years –

under the thumb
so long! We don't give two hoots!

Fed up. Ready to rouse
a mews. It was no fair exchange.

## VIII  A Lanner Falcon Called Tisiphone

Tisiphone sits
fierce as a harpy
but rendered
blind as Phineus
by her hood.
She is just as wise.
Her name
is germinating.
She preens
her plumes
and wills them brass
like those birds
which bred by
Lake Stymphalia.
Her cry can
shred silence.
Her talons
are sharp still
and for the air alone.
Her master, he grows old.
Only the opportunity
is wanting.

# REFRAIN

Better than a partridge in a pear tree,
you give me three pairs of nesting nightingales
and it's not even Christmas.

Snug as oak thicket
where they hid their speckled eggs
you gentled them in your head for a month

until I could make them sing
in my mind's ear with the range
and versatility for which they're famous.

How is it then
that you reduce me
to the same old song?

# SNOW, THE FIRST TIME

Once green gave way to gold, and more light
was lost, by chance they came to what had been
the garden. It was so changed they did not
know the place. As the chill of night
crept forward  and the leaves fell, trees
were no longer shelter. So they found a cave.

Under the constellation of the crab
he skinned a bear, using its claw to strip
the thick pelt clear. He'd come upon it lifeless.
(Before they fled, some animals had grown
fierce and dusk brought strange cries.)

None of the birds would touch the windfalls
from a tree that looked familiar. An acrid smoke
coiled from the apple wood as it refused
to flame. The cold unsheathed its claws.
They woke to an odd glare. Everything
was white. More feathers floated down.

The stream was silent. He slipped on the bank
and flung his arms out wide. And when he stood
they froze at the shape imprinted on the snow.
And stared, until a sharp wind drove them back.

# PAINTER

Late August we absorb in different ways:
I reach for words to chime with what I see;
your harmonies are of a different kind,
all shape and shade. We're picking sloes,
the sheen of each fruit misted
with a premonition of the cold to come.

Autumn, furtive pointillist,
is creeping in – dots of hawthorn berries
ripe before their time; the flicker
of rogue red hips deep in the hedge.

But what seeps into you
is that vast expanse of ever-changing blue
swept by scudding cirrus, stratocumulus
whose sibilance, almost without you knowing,
is whispering at your fingers.

When you reach home you will
retouch that problematic sky.

# PASSING

She says her eyes aren't good now –
it's something new in the exchange
we have each time we coincide
when I'm out with the dog.

These days she only ventures up the drive
and with a walking frame. Quite often
she'll be sitting on the wall.
*How old is he?* I tell her
every time. And we go through all
the dogs she's owned and how
*they know you're doggy*
when she bends to pat
the ones whose owners try
to hurry past her gate.

This morning I jog by at 6 a.m.
Her lights are on. She's staring
through the window into a beyond
where they all are – the bull mastiff
*I had at three months old;*
the numerous Dalmatians;
those dogs she judged at Cruft's.

The trees are turning; Winter's
in the wings of birds who feel
the pull of somewhere else
now days are shortening.

And sometime soon she'll be there
at the very moment when the night
meets day and dark will be subsumed.

# FROST

At eighty when you let your hair turn silver
(your eyebrows holding out) you froze at cameras;
waved us away impatiently on birthdays.
Not like that woman whose classic profile
stares from my study wall in black and white.
She let herself be led from Fawcett Street
up to a studio at an unknown
photographer's request – so daring then.
Her beauty's evident; the bloom preserved.
But there's a dignity that winter brings:
when frost translates a landscape, clean and stark,
summer's eclipsed. And should ice embrace fire
its essence is too elusive to be caught
by the cold December sun's relentless lens.

# JOKULSARLON

The evening of your passing
we stopped to watch a flock of whooper swans:
so many white shapes gracing the wide bay they would
have been impossible to count.

Because the museum closed at six and English time
ticked on beyond me I can pinpoint the moment you
crossed over. It caught up with me next morning when,
impossibly, the sun came slanting through the window of my room
just as the phone rang.

That day we sailed on the lagoon
where the great glacier Vatnajokull,
has slowly rolled its tongue back.

I'm offered words of comfort – someone's brother back in Oz
and miles from help, is bitten by a redback. He drives and drives.
Against all odds the medics bring him round. Later he tells
how his two uncles (who had been dead some years) urged him on.

I focus on the shapes the glacier's calved and see the small ones
are melting into swans – stretching their necks across
their arching backs. And I think of the picture
that will be hanging in the kitchen by your chair:

a flock of sleeping swans dusted with white,
one in the foreground
sloughing off the ice.

To face a morning.

# TAKING OFF

How was I to know that, discarding your stick, you'd one
foot on the runway before I'd reached Stansted

psyching up for take-off. I called you from the departure
lounge. It was the summer of the 2008 Olympics; I flew

to a land of ice and pumice. Imagined what you'd say
when I brought you rainbows wrested from the air

by thrashing waters. And tiny blooms, against all odds,
starring the lava fields - when I was small and you led me

to the bus stop in Moor Lane, you'd point out flowers
thrusting through tarmac and marvel at their strength.

How did you move so fast? As you approached the line
I saw the swans - paler than angels - exchange

their element for air, running on water
until they rose to grace. You hated deathbed scenes.

Have they the power to reconcile, my pictures
of those frail defiant constellations rising from the ash?

# GEESE

don't wait to be frozen out:
before the ice can get a grip they rise
above it all, wind up

what's left of summer:
a skein unspools across the sky,
unfazed by limitless ocean,

forming a seamless dart;
the selfless leader needles ahead
unafraid to drop back,

each bird a stitch
in the victory – each one part
of that fluid nib that,

with the blueprint of instinct
still unclouded and with a will
beyond the corporate

writes its destiny across
the heavens, wheeling down fortune
or the fate that cuts the thread.

# MY FEET WON'T TOUCH THE GROUND

Based on the folk belief swifts had no feet,
in heraldry these birds became the arms
of the fourth son for whom land was a dream.
But he was unconfined, could take control.
No need to chase or chastise lazy serfs
or be caught up in schemes of snaring dames
or rut in wedlock for elusive sons.
Free to cross a sea or two and make a name.
Next time my thoughts are tending to alight
on one who would confine me to the earth,
I'll think of young swifts roosting on the wing –
dark stars that drift with ease on August nights,
by day screaming and diving. And who are
always exultant, ever on the wing.

# FREDDIE AND THE TREECREEPER

In his cupped hands the bird,
each feature perfect: curved beak
white breast, back flecked with brown.
*It flew into our classroom window.*

It's still warm – little tree mouse
who scurried after insects on the bark
in a jiggish dot-to-dot. *Treecreeper*
I say, knowing it's just 'a bird' to him –

when once he would have known its shape
and names like linnet, dunnock, redpoll,
would call up cries and eggs and dipping flights.
At least their nests are safe now.

He lays it beneath the hedge *in case
it comes to*. I know it will not stir.
But then next day he asks,
*Miss, what was that bird again?*

# THE RIGHT WORDS

After months in the far north
they return, like snow buntings
in a blizzard of wings. I did not
think they could thrive in icy climes,
but here they are, searching the wrackline
for drifted seed. When they turned pale,
fell between a rock

and a barren place, they lay
deep in a corrie in a nest lined
with sheep's wool, fur
from a mountain hare.
And down from a ptarmigan
conferring resilience,
its chameleon gift.

# ALL THE BIRDS HAVE FLOWN

If I'd thought of you in that old folks' home
on the coast road, big picture windows facing
out to sea, you wouldn't have been that side
of the glass, but on the cliffs, charting a flock of dunlin
or listening for the redshank's clamorous cry.
And when weak eyes reduced all long-legged birds
to some species of wader, you would still pick out
an oystercatcher, red bill probing
the bladderwrack – bifocal friendly,
striking black and white. It couldn't be
you huddled in that chair, back to the light,
oblivious to the bittersweet of sunsets,
unable to tell a hawk from a handsaw
whichever way the cruel wind was blowing.